STORIES
OF HOPE

STORIES
OF HOPE

IGNATIAN SPIRITUALITY PROJECT

First Printing, 2016

ISBN-13: 9780692630938
ISBN-10: 0692630937
Library of Congress Control Number: 2016932425

Ignatian Spirituality Project
1641 South Allport Street
Chicago, IL 60608

http://www.ignatianspiritualityproject.org

"The eyes of his soul were opened ...
From that day everything appeared in a new light."

ST. IGNATIUS LOYOLA, *AUTOBIOGRAPHY*

PREFACE

Since 1998, when the first Ignatian Spirituality Project (ISP) retreat for those experiencing homelessness and recovering from addiction took place, we have heard countless powerful and transformational stories from our retreatants and our volunteer facilitators. These stories speak both to the darkness that many of our retreatants have gone through and the light that they have found by (re)encountering God or their Higher Power. All of the stories ultimately point to the hope found on an Ignatian retreat.

ISP has developed a retreat model that cares for the interior and spiritual lives of those living with homelessness and suffering from addiction. Blending elements of Ignatian Spirituality and the 12-step recovery program, ISP retreats are an effective resource in laying a foundation of hope, community and healing for those living on the margins. By offering a safe space in which to share their stories, our retreatants come to see that they are not alone in their struggles, that they are loved both by God and by those on retreat with them.

On a typical retreat, about 12 retreatants join 4 volunteer facilitators at a retreat center for a day and a half. There are opportunities for all participants, retreatants and facilitators alike, to share with one another about their struggles, their hopes, and their own experience of God or their Higher Power. There are also times set aside for personal prayer and reflection. Because they are non-denominational in nature, we say that our retreats are spiritual but not religious.

As our Co-Founder Fr. Bill Creed, SJ said early on, "we can provide an endless supply of material resources to the poor and marginalized, but there can be no real transition from poverty until the individual person has the inner resources to make different choices." ISP fosters these inner resources. For many, the retreat is the spark that leads to long-term transformation and an end to homelessness, thus altering the cycle of despair and loneliness that has kept so many of our retreatants out of right relationship with themselves, others, and God—and kept them on the streets.

In the past 18 years ISP has grown substantially. As of 2016, there are now over 800 ISP volunteers offering retreats in 29 cities in the United States and Canada. We are proud to share with you the following Stories of Hope from across our network.

Camille Devaney
Board Chair

Tom Drexler
Executive Director

TABLE OF CONTENTS

GOD

COMMUNITY

HEALING

INTRODUCTION

Fr. Bill Creed, SJ
*Co-Founder of the Ignatian
Spirituality Project*

Too many men and women in our society live in a world of darkness—the darkness of homelessness, the darkness of addiction, the darkness of loneliness. We all face moments of darkness in our lives, but for some, those moments can turn into a lifetime.

The Ignatian Spirituality Project (ISP) is founded on the conviction that a way out of the darkness exists. That way is HOPE. Hope awakens a new sense of self, a self who can choose not to be fatalistic but who can re-imagine a vibrant life. Hope opens a life of meaning.

From its beginning, ISP has appealed to the heart and center of the human person by creating a community of hope. Homeless men and women in recovery join together on retreat with volunteer facilitators to form a new community. This new community is founded on a shared commitment to the spiritual journey and the non-judgmental sharing with one another of our own sacred stories. Whatever our background, whatever our current situation, we all have fears and struggles, we all have hopes and dreams. In sharing these struggles and hopes with our fellow retreatants, we both grow closer to one another and grow in our relationship to God or our Higher Power.

Within the ISP community, retreatants and volunteers alike begin to see themselves and their future with new eyes. The dynamic of hope draws people out of themselves. We become friends with people we have never before encountered in such a close way—men and women who once were lost on the streets, trapped in addiction and homelessness, but who now flourish and are giving back; men and women who have lived in relative affluence and who now spend time with those on the margins of society. We find that below the superficial differences of our lives, below the societal barriers between us, our common humanity runs deep. We find a new purpose in belonging to the ISP community, a community which teems with hope.

The origins of ISP are rooted in God's hope, God's dream, for humanity. St. Paul in writing to the people in Rome said, "Rejoice in hope" (Rom 12:12). In the pages which follow, you will encounter women and men who constitute this ISP community of hope. That encounter will fill you with joy—the joy fostered by hope.

PEACE

14. What did you learn about yourself?

That I now have an inner peace that I've never known could exist.

- Retreatant in New Orleans, LA

What did you learn about yourself?

I learned to be at peace with myself and to feel happiness, love, and warmth. Also I know now that my light will shine again and brighter

- Retreatant in Dayton, OH

AN OVERWHELMING FEELING OF PEACE

Amanda Asque
Chicago, IL

I showed up at the St. Martin De Porres House of Hope recovery home on the South Side of Chicago lifeless, penniless and hopeless. I continued to stay there because I had nowhere else to go. I had severed every family tie. I had almost lost the will to live. Through the midst of all of that I went to sleep at 15 and woke up at the age of 38, addicted to heroin for 23 years. I started using as a child and when I woke up in active addiction I was 38 years old. I stayed in the darkness for 23 years. The funny part is, I ran away from home because I was scared and I stayed in the streets because I was too terrified to go back home.

While I was at St. Martin's, I didn't talk to anyone and I didn't want anyone to talk to me. "Can't you see I'm in pain? Can't you see I don't like it here? Can't you see I don't like you? Can't you see I don't like myself?" I was stoic and rude.

In 2006, I was aggravated. I didn't appreciate being picked to be on a spiritual retreat. It came at a time when I was my most broken, fractured self. I was just beginning to realize that I was the one who got me here. I was pissed. Sister Therese from St. Martin's said it was time for a spiritual retreat and I resisted. Some of the ISP volunteers and Sr. Therese tricked me by telling me that I would love it. I thought they were trying to pull one over on me. She asked me to go because she saw how broken I was. All she did was show me love. The more love she showed me the more I didn't want it. I forgot how to feel. I forgot social graces.

As we travelled to the retreat, I remember being in the car and being really quiet and I remember the scenery, it brought me to some semblance of calm. My mind was going a thousand miles a minute and the uncertainty about where I was going made me scared. But as we were driving the beauty of the scenery calmed me and when we arrived the grounds were beautiful. It was amazing.

The retreat icebreaker for me was the partner introduction. Laura Howard, one of the retreat facilitators, shared authentically about herself and I found that charismatic. To her, it wasn't about race, social background, or anything like that. It was about sharing our hopes, dreams, aspirations and emotional vulnerabilities. I felt like I was important. She also shared her own questions and vulnerabilities. I never thought we could have things in common. I thought, "maybe there is something to this." And that was the icebreaker for me, because she came from such an authentic place. It was not because it resembled what I had gone through. It wasn't gritty or grimy but it was real and it resonated with me.

I began to feel safe. It was an overwhelming feeling of peace. I didn't know anybody there so I wasn't afraid of anybody. The welcoming spirit of the retreat house and the genuine concern and care of the team members made me feel safe. You could feel their warm energy. Not to mention the food was incredible. It was like food for the spirit, food for the mind and food for the body. You were fed all the way around and you felt it. You felt food.

It was like, "wait a minute—they care about us? They know we stole, we were raped, we were molested and they still cared?! Where is the camera? Is this real? God is in ALL of this?" They gave me a place to share. I had never shared my story before. I shared things I thought I was going to go to the grave with. I wasn't going to share my deep, dark secrets. Before the retreat I didn't trust nothing or nobody. Because I was just hurt every time I did. Before this retreat, I did NOT like feeling vulnerable. But on the retreat I got in touch with places in my consciousness that had been uninhabited for a LONG time. I felt human on this retreat. Before I started making the

ISP retreat, I had no idea how intricate my spirituality was. I was ashamed about everything and I had no idea how to be anything besides ashamed.

After the retreat, Sr. Therese said I looked different. Everything I learned on the retreat and with the retreat team was like a huge chest of spiritual tools that I took back to the shelter and to my life and to the women and to their children and the staff. Everyone wins if just one person comes back different and they are exposed to that one person.

After the retreat I started taking ownership and started addressing my feelings. I understood that I had to feel the feelings; I didn't have to react to them. I started behaving constructively over a period of time. It happened over a five-month period and after that St. Martin's offered me a job. I also took care of my 88-year-old grandmother, after 14 months clean. I would NEVER have done that without the support of the community I found on that first retreat. From there I began to get involved with the ISP Women's retreat team, sharing my witness on the retreats. I was honored and shocked. I was never shunned or judged. They wanted me to share. Now as the team's witness coordinator, I have the chance to help other women who are experiencing homelessness and recovery to share their own stories on ISP retreats.

FINDING THE PEACE
INSIDE

Jimi Fardan
Baltimore, MD

I attended my first ISP retreat in the fall of 2007. It was the very first Baltimore ISP retreat. I was in a long-term treatment and recovery program and my counselor told me that he thought that I would be a good candidate. I had no prior knowledge of retreats.

I was a little skeptical as it sounded like a religious retreat. I thought it would be proselytizing. Nonetheless, because of where I was and the people I was around, I was willing to try new things. I had been sober for about eight months and I felt like I was in a good place to try it.

I knew I would be away for one night but that was ALL I knew. I didn't know who I was going with, where I was going or what we would be doing. At that time, I didn't worry about it. I trusted the director of my program—they had never pointed me in the wrong direction and I knew it would not be to my detriment. I was confused but I had an open spirit.

Confusion was the first thing I felt. The other part was that I thought it was some more of the same BS. That changed when I met Wayne Richard and Fr. Bill Creed, SJ, who were helping to lead the retreat. Fr. Creed impressed me. When he opened his mouth he was not proselytizing, he was talking about where I wanted to go.

The exercises brought that out. The "Fear and Trust" exercise allowed me to be open. During that exercise Wayne and I connected and I realized that maybe I could be open with this group. I was impressed by this big guy. He was alright. I am still friends with Wayne. His positive energy made me pay attention because I wanted to have that as well. We did more in a relaxing day on retreat than I would have done at the recovery house.

At the end of the day I felt good and turned on to the program. With the way that the energy was flowing, I felt invigorated and excited and looked forward to what would happen next. I had a thousand questions. What would happen after Bill and Wayne left and went back to Chicago?

I had arrived at the recovery house because I had given up most things in my life to continue using drugs. It was bit by bit, but eventually it became a full-time job. Since I was a veteran, my wife and I had gone to the VA to enroll me in a program. After leaving, it didn't take me a week to start using again. They gave me options but they weren't the ones I wanted. I went to this program twice and by the time I got to the retreat, I had been to four different recovery programs.

What was different on the ISP retreat was that I had begun to look at myself. I realized that I was responsible for everything in my life. I was the common denominator. Life didn't happen to me, I happened to it. Until I looked at myself and realized I was trying to live my life without any principles at all, I could not recover. Some of the things that I held were truly false. Some of the things that I had to let go of hurt. What I saw wasn't pretty but it was me and I had to work on what was real. I had to be accountable for what I did. I had to take personal responsibility for my life and I was trying to do this when I went on retreat.

I thought I was going to leave all of the bonding and beauty that I had found on retreat at the retreat house, but what I found was that that peace was actually inside of me. What I found on the retreat was inside of my soul and it was helping me to sustain myself. As a result of learning how to sit still with myself on the retreat, I was able to find myself and find that peace. Sue Cesare, who had organized the retreat, helped me to reconnect and remember that. She and Wayne fed my spirit. It helped me to keep what I had found on retreat as a part of my life after the retreat was over.

Sue asked me to be a witness on the next retreat. I got to know the rest of the ISP team and they taught me how to share with other men how the retreat had affected me. It was what I needed at the right time. I have been involved with the team now for several years. The ISP retreat gives every retreatant hope. All of them. The ones who are witnesses, the ones who only attend once, the ones who aren't ready. It gives each of them hope.

Jimi Fardan's artwork is available through his website, www.pencilmania.net.

FEELING GOD'S
PRESENCE AND PEACE

Ennis Adams
Indianapolis, IN

God often works in mysterious ways and in my life that's exactly what happened. When I was at my lowest point, after a life of drinking, using drugs, being incarcerated, living on the streets and being close to death, God rescued me and helped me turn my life around. God came to me through the care and help of another person, my good friend Leo. He believed in me, challenged me and never gave up on me. Because of Leo, and the power of God working through him, I have been transformed and I am now able to help others who are ready to give up on themselves.

When I was a child and teenager, growing up in Indianapolis, I began hanging out with the wrong crowd, experimenting with drugs and drinking. My mom raised me, my three brothers and two sisters by herself, so I didn't have a male role model in my life as I was growing up. I spent a lot of time out of the house on the streets. Eventually I got myself into a lot of trouble and ended up spending five and a half years at the Pendleton Juvenile Correctional Facility, where I finished high school and learned three different trades.

When I got out, I married my high school sweetheart and we had three children. During this time, I was working, helping take care of the kids and going to church, but I was living a double life. I was going through the motions of life but I always found time to hang out on the streets and do drugs on a daily basis. I tried to make it all work together—my job, taking care of the kids, going to church and doing drugs, but something had to give. It eventually caught up to me and I found myself back in prison and separated from my family.

This time, when I got out, it was even worse than before. I went right back to the streets and although I worked a lot, I never had any permanent job. I lived in the streets, drank alcohol and did drugs regularly and got farther and farther away from my family. This became my way of life and the years kept going by.

Eventually, I began working a recovery program at St. Vincent de Paul and going to church, but once again I was only going through the motions. Leo was volunteering at St. Vincent de Paul and this is where he and I met and became friends. Leo offered to help me but I wasn't ready to share with him because I wasn't being honest with myself. I wanted to work a program, go to church and continue drinking all at the same time but it didn't work and I ended up in the hospital, very sick. Finally, at this time, I decided that this was it.

I got out of the hospital and began working my program with honesty and sincerity. Leo was right there to help me, hiring me as a day laborer for a construction project and then eventually keeping me on as a permanent employee. I was so grateful for his compassion and concern. I soon found out that he was a member of the men's ISP team and I was eager to go when he invited me on a retreat.

I had never experienced as much peace as I did on my first ISP overnight retreat. It was a beautiful feeling. The people that I met and the stories that I heard were so similar to mine. I couldn't believe it! I thought I was the only one going through all of this stuff. The retreat strengthened me in so many ways. I felt God's presence and peace and it helped me to continue in my sobriety. I decided that I wanted more of that feeling so I decided to join ISP myself and become a witness for future retreats. Now I am working alongside Leo, telling my story to other men who go on the retreats. By telling my story, I feel as if God is working through me to help them, just like God worked through Leo to help me.

Once, I was ashamed of my story, but now I am happy to let God work through me and share it with others. My life is so different now than it was when I was using and living on the streets. I live in my own home; I have a job that I love, working with Leo's company; I am a member of the ISP team; I have many friends; and best of all, I have a great relationship with all three of my children. And for the icing on the cake… all three of them are college graduates and I couldn't be prouder!

I thank my friend, Leo, for being God's hands, feet, eyes and ears to me. Because of his love, I have been transformed. I want to do the same for other people now and I hope God will use me, the way he used Leo, to make a difference in this world.

LIKE A PERFECT PEACE

Tywana Lewis
New Orleans, LA

I am in recovery from heroin and crack addiction. While caught up in my addiction, I was living anywhere the night would catch me. I was using all my money for drugs. I was selling my body for money or a place to stay.

I went to my first ISP retreat in August 2011 when I was in the treatment center at Grace House. I was already trying to form a relationship with the God of my understanding. It was perfect timing. It was a very moving experience for me as far as learning how to meditate.

Leading up to the retreat, I was so excited, I looked at it as God-sent. I was trying to get that closer connection with God so this was like icing on the cake. My first few hours on retreat, the first thing that caught my attention was the peace, the quiet, the calm. Everything was still, but a pleasant still. Everybody had this calmness and this peace. You did not hear any distractions, it was like a perfect peace.

The meditations were very helpful. It taught me how to talk to God. It was simple. You didn't have to go through long, complicated prayers. It was a more open-minded form of communication with God for me.

On the retreat I learned that I am a stronger woman than I thought I was. I have the willingness to go on. People tend to see things in you that you cannot see in yourself. The retreat helped me to look at things from other people's point of view. It made me look at myself more as a woman in recovery.

After graduating from Grace House, I started working at a Pinkberry Yogurt store, and soon became an Assistant General Manager. I was struggling to figure out how to be a respectable but assertive manager. Because of the retreat I could see my strength and God's presence. It gave me wisdom and understanding. I could notice God in certain things that I would never have been able to see before.

I went back on several retreats as a witness, to share my story with other women in recovery. I got a full understanding of my role as a witness when I saw light come back into someone's eyes. I work at Grace House, where many of the retreatants come from, and I can see how much of a change occurs on retreat. I get to see the women change and support them in that change.

My GM at Pinkberry would say that every time I came back from a retreat I had a glow about me. Every time I came back, it gave me a bit more strength to go a little further. It's like getting my battery recharged.

I am now GM at my own Pinkberry store, and I still participate in ISP retreats when I can.

I FELT AT PEACE

Ernestine Borders
Milwaukee, WI

A few years ago, I was staying at a Salvation Army shelter in Milwaukee and my case manager suggested that I go on a retreat with the Ignatian Spirituality Project. At the time, I had been in recovery for more than six months. It was my first retreat, and I was excited about getting out of the shelter. Before going on the retreat I had never experienced a spiritual awakening. After the retreat, I felt big doors had opened wide in my heart. On the retreat, I heard a witness share her story. I felt it was such a blessing. It made me want to share my story.

My parents were both alcoholics. I had my first drink at 12 years old. At 26 years old I started using cocaine. I used until I was 50 years old. In November of 1992, on Thanksgiving, I was abducted off the street and taken into a building. A man threw me out the window and then raped me. My head was swollen to the size of two heads. My left leg was twisted the wrong way. I was not able to do anything for myself. Someone had to feed me, bathe me and I was not even allowed painkillers because of my drug use.

Even this experience would not stop me from using. I continued to use until I became homeless. I was sleeping on porches and in abandoned cars. I was going to Heart to Heart and getting Walmart certificates, which I sold, using the money to purchase drugs. I had fallen into the cocaine crisis and no matter what I did I couldn't break the cycle.

Someone asked me if I wanted help and I finally said yes. This caring woman wrote a letter and got me into a treatment center. In the treatment center, I had a wake-up call from God. This was on August 19, 2006 and I have not used drugs since.

I had never had a spiritual awakening, but in 2009 it happened when I experienced my first ISP retreat. The retreat center was so calming and relaxing. I felt peace the moment I walked in the door. Before the retreat, I did a lot of praying to prepare and asked God to lead my words, so I was not too nervous or scared. The spirit just led me.

On the retreat we talked about fear. When I was asked what my fear was, I said, "I have no fear since God lifted me up." Two hours later, I went to the chapel and I experienced fear. Tears just came to me and I had to ask for forgiveness. I'm not sure what God did to me but I felt a burden being lifted off my shoulders. When I came back to the group, God gave me confirmation of His presence through that fear. He comforted me and let me know He was there on that retreat. I must have cried a half bucket of tears. The tears were burning my face but it was the Lord touching me again.

I felt like tons of weight was lifted up off of me after the retreat. I felt at peace. I felt like I took a big stretch of every bone in my body. I felt real good about myself and about telling my story. I believe that God led the ISP women to the shelter to bring me forth and express the terrible things that happened while I was using drugs and the beautiful things that happened when I let go and let God.

The presence of God was there on that ISP retreat. It is the only way I can explain my experience. I had space to share my story and I realized it made a difference. After the retreat, I found myself laughing more. Laughter from the stomach. I had never had something to laugh about. The retreat opened me up and helped me find life again.

HOPE

15. How did this retreat impact your spiritual/recovery journey?

It inspired me and gave me hope to be able to stay sober and it made my faith in God stronger.

– Retreatant in Washington, DC

14. What did you learn about yourself?

I have hope for my future

– Retreatant in Providence, RI

I HAVE NOW EXPERIENCED HOPE

Rene Petaway
Washington, DC

I was born in New York in 1948. My mother left me in the hospital. My father's mother brought me home and raised me. My mother and father were supposed to get married but my mother found out he was a bigamist, so that didn't take place. I was raised by my grandparents. My grandfather was not happy with the fact that my grandmother took on the responsibility because they were in their 50s at the time. My mother lived in Baltimore but never kept in contact with me until I was about 13 or 14, so I could babysit my siblings.

I had my first drink when I was nine years old in the basement of Calvary Baptist Church, helping my grandmother with the communion trays. My drinking in junior high school kicked up a notch but I never considered myself a drunk. When I turned 15, I stopped going to church because I wasn't getting anything from it.

I got married very early, as soon as I turned 18. I moved to Connecticut with my husband and I had my daughter when I was 20. My husband was addicted to drugs. My marriage lasted about seven years. After my divorce, I started really drinking a lot, but never falling off of barstools or anything like that. I worked as a teacher's aide for 18 years at a place called Boys Village that worked with homeless children. I raised my daughter and sent her away to college.

My daughter married and moved to Washington, DC. She called me when I was about to retire and asked me to come and help her out with the kids, because she wanted to go back to work. So I came to DC in 2007 and stayed with my daughter. After two or three months my daughter talked to me about my drinking. I told her to mind her business, I'm fine. Three months after that, my son-in-law called me and said not to pick the kids up from daycare, and that when they got home, they wanted me gone.

I had a little money saved up from my pension, and I had a car, so I left. I stayed in hotels and motels, and then I went to Baltimore, where my mother lived. I felt like she owed me something in life. When I asked her if I could come and stay with her, she replied, "Absolutely not." I was crushed and ended up staying in a rooming house, which got raided by the police, and I was just lost.

I called my daughter and said, "I'm not trying to break up your marriage but I need you to help me out. Send me some money, talk to your husband, or something." A colleague of hers had told her about a women's shelter called N Street Village, and that's where I ended up, in 2009. I had to go to 90 meetings in 90 days, get a sponsor, all of this stuff. In my mind I was thinking I can do all of this, but only until they find me an apartment and they refer me to a job some place. I still was not dealing with my addiction.

That December, a friend at N Street invited me to go to an ISP retreat. I wasn't up for hearing a lot of preaching and praying, that's not my thing. So she asked me if I would just go to support her. We'd become pretty close so I went with her. We got to Loyola Retreat House, which was on this beautiful land, everything was quiet and peaceful. After living in a dorm with nine other women on cots eight and a half inches apart from each other, it was a beautiful thing to have my own room and bath, and the food was amazing.

The retreat was an amazing experience. One thing I witnessed while I was there—early, early morning there was this huge eagle, the wingspan was enormous, it was almost fearful to watch it, but I'd never seen anything like that. And I was 60 years old. Hearing other women share while I was there—one woman was sharing about her relationship with her mother, how rocky it was. I was able to quickly identify in. Another woman shared that her mother had passed and how much she missed her. It made me go inside and think, why am I holding this resentment?

The Ignatian Spirituality Project has allowed me to learn how to meditate and learn how to pray. I knew the regular prayers and I always used to pray to God, "Get me out of this mess," "Help me find my way," things of that nature. But I learned through ISP that when you pray you're at peace with God, you're building a relationship with God. The more I pray to God in a thankful, grateful way, the better my life is.

Experiencing these retreats has made me a totally different, better person. When I got back I was able to meet with my mother, express to her my true feelings. Things she told me were just amazing. She did the best she could do. That was a better choice for her at that time. We made amends and have a great relationship today.

Learning how to meditate and pray was a big deal for me. I now have a relationship with God, and I got it from a lot of the exercises that ISP does when we go on retreats. I've learned how to be a witness, I've learned how to have more compassion, in terms of listening to someone else's pain, I've learned how to walk through things and not be in fear, which is a big relief. I figured that God would never forgive me for all the things I've done throughout my life. But apparently He is a very forgiving God. It's just been really awesome. I have now experienced HOPE (Happiness, Opportunity, Peace & Empowerment).

I now have my own apartment and a job as an administrative assistant at the Festival Center. I also spread the word to the new women at N Street Village. I still go back there and volunteer. I go back to give back, leading a weekly anger management program.

I enjoy going back on ISP retreats as a witness, bringing HOPE to others. A lot of the women from N Street who attended retreats that I went to, the change in them was like night and day. I recall an incident where some of the women, when they were going to the courtyard at N Street to smoke a cigarette, they'd be cursing up a breeze. And these same women, after returning from the retreat, you didn't hear any foul mouth, talking about each other. It became more of a sisterhood, they were just at peace.

SHARING HOPE

Amanda Lisle
Akron, OH

S ome of Amanda's earliest memories are of growing up in a house "where we sat down to dinner every night." However, at the age of 12, Amanda found out that the man she had always thought was her father was not, and her whole sense of family changed. She bounced from house to house, staying with grandma, and a couple of aunts. With so much upheaval in her life, she learned to manipulate others at an early age. She didn't entirely dislike the moving around; there were cousins to play with and she was drawn to the adults. Amanda recalls Friday night poker when the family members played cards, drank, and sometimes smoked dope. She liked hanging out in the kitchen, and liked being around the smoking and drinking. At school she only did just enough to pass.

By the age of 13, Amanda was drinking wine coolers with her mom, and by 14 was drinking Mad Dog for the express purpose of getting drunk. Amanda hung out with older kids and recalls that she "didn't fit in her skin" and wanted to be older. Her first daughter was born when she was 16. When she became pregnant, she decided she had to grow up, and stopped using alcohol and drugs. She moved in with the baby's father and dropped out of the tenth grade, but did complete her GED after the baby was born.

By 20, Amanda had a five-year-old daughter and a new baby, but was feeling increasingly depressed about her life. Although she and the children's father originally rented a house, they ended up living in the projects. By 21, Amanda had kicked out her boyfriend. Although she always made sure her daughters were safe, Amanda began to spend Wednesday nights partying, then Saturday nights, and finally Wednesday, Friday and Saturday nights. During this period of time, Amanda first tried meth, and was immediately hooked. She began to sell it so she could use for free. After her mother's death, she started to take prescription pills. Finally, "to get away from the mess," she moved to Florida, where she picked up a criminal case.

Amanda came home to Akron and moved into the basement of her father's house, with her father and children living upstairs. Her children's father moved into the house as well. Amanda started using intravenous drugs, spending most of her time locked in the basement so her daughters would not see her using. She was not available to her children, she was now on probation, and had a couple of criminal cases for driving under the influence and possession of drug paraphernalia. She was doing everything to excess, and the Children's Service Bureau had been called about her daughters. Her probation officer asked her, "What are you doing? You are going to die." Amanda was given the choice of going to jail or to treatment. She also had a choice of leaving the house herself or having the children and their father leave the house. She left.

At 30, Amanda was living in garages. She used synthetic drugs to pass her detox tests. She had no kids, no home, and there was a waiting list to get into addiction treatment. Finally, on June 28th, 2011, Amanda entered a 72-day treatment program. After completing the program, she was admitted to a two-year transitional living program. Only three weeks later, she met a guy with drugs and quickly relapsed. She called AA, got a sponsor, and "through the grace of God" was able to keep her housing. Two weeks after the relapse, still not having custody of her kids, Amanda was invited to attend an ISP retreat.

The ISP retreat came at just the right time. She remembers the retreat as "being separated from everything and sharing hope." She did not talk about her relapse there, but felt a connection with the other women. Through writing a Letter to God and journaling she began to see how God was working in her life.

At 11 months sober, Amanda came on a second ISP retreat as the witness, and shared her story with the group. In thinking about how things had changed for her in the past year, Amanda felt that she could offer hope to the new women. Since then, she has joined the Akron ISP team. "Being a part of ISP has changed my life," she says.

Amanda's life today is very different from what it was. In four years she has gone from not having her children, not having housing, and not having a driver's license to having a full-time job, an apartment, and not being on probation. Her older daughter is in college, and her younger daughter, who lives with her, is a straight-A student in high school. Amanda has a driver's license and a car. She is engaged to be married.

Amanda feels that ISP gave her a better connection to God, and nourishing that connection has given her the life she has today. Amanda not only has hope for herself, she shares her hope with others.

LAYING A FOUNDATION OF HOPE

James Hanna
Pittsburgh, PA

Men finish an ISP retreat weekend with more than they arrived with. While each man is affected differently, there is one thing that each of us has more of at the end of the retreat than at the beginning: hope.

It has been my privilege to be associated with the ISP retreat team for three years. The ISP mission statement includes the phrase "laying a foundation of hope which can lead to further and long-lasting transformation." I have seen this foundation laid on each of our retreats—and I have been a beneficiary, too.

When my friend Tom first approached me a few years ago to help launch ISP in Pittsburgh I didn't know what to expect. I certainly didn't expect the many blessings received.

The blessings begin with the men I get to meet—both those we serve and fellow retreat team members. The stories we share immerse me in reality; there is no escaping "living life on life's terms" and the men bring this honesty to the retreat. They help ground me in authenticity, and this gives me hope.

On each retreat, even though we come with so many different life stories, backgrounds, and from different locations, there is a fraternal air that develops quickly, a solidarity that binds us; we are all in this together. They help me recognize that none of us are alone, that we are one human family, and this gives me hope.

Over the past three years, on each retreat, when men reflect on their relationship with God they remind me that we are all, each one of us, created in the image and likeness of God. They remind me that God wishes for us to be in right relationship with God, with each other, and with our own self, and this gives me hope.

Being part of the ISP retreat team has provided me with positive experiences that I would otherwise not have had, has introduced me to amazing men I would not have otherwise met, and has improved my spiritual life in a way I could not have imagined, and all of this fills me with gratitude.

REDISCOVERING HOPE

John Lynch
Pittsburgh, PA

John Lynch is a man with two stories of hope. In the first instance, he was not able to sustain hope and it evaporated, leaving him with a life of addiction, criminality and depression. Then, in 2006, while in prison, John says that God removed his obsession, and he became convinced that he deserved a good life and another way to live. Through AA, and the ISP retreats, John has re-discovered hope, and has indeed found another way to live.

John was born with an arteriovenous malformation (AVM) deep in his brain. This condition resulted in seizures, and there was a constant risk of blood vessel rupture. In 1987, John became the first person in North America to undergo Gamma Knife surgery, performed by Dr. Lunsford in Pittsburgh, which gave him hope and another chance at life. John was 27 at the time, but had been in addiction since his early teens. He could neither fully understand nor appreciate this chance he'd been given, and was not able to build on the hope that this groundbreaking surgery provided.

John now lives at St. Joseph's House of Hospitality in Pittsburgh and has been sober for eight years. He credits the ISP retreats for having helped renew his hope. John had attended AA retreats before he participated in an ISP retreat. Nonetheless, the ISP retreat surprised him. "The people all shared, and didn't hold back. They got along and were there for each other. There was no-one left in the background." The setting for the retreat was "like a vacation." He was able to share in the small group "with no stress."

In maintaining his sobriety, John is interested in exploring more than one avenue. While appreciating AA and NA, he finds that "ISP is unique; it's a new beginning for people with drug and alcohol problems." John has since participated in other ISP retreats, and has served on the team as a witness. He feels that, "I'm going to be involved for the rest of my life. I'm going to stay at St. Joe's a long time."

Today, John has goals in his life. He very much wants to be part of a process to help people; he wants to give back. "Helping others helps me, it helps me grow. I keep things by giving them away." The things John desires today are trust and respect, and he earns those by driving a van, helping in the St. Joe's store, helping in the kitchen, serving on the ISP team. He's an example to others.

How did ISP help kindle and feed this hope? "It lit a fire, I'm more driven, I'm working the program," John says. "The people who run ISP are really caring, giving, they make you comfortable, they don't look down on you. I'm comfortable instead of awkward. I feel good after I witness. It reaffirms that I'm moving forward and strengthens my relationship with God."

John Lynch is a man who was twice given hope, once through surgery and once through faith. The surgery enabled him to live; the faith makes his life worth living.

LOVE

14. What did you learn about yourself?

That I am worth loving.

- Retreatant in Houston, TX

What did you learn about yourself?

THAT I LOVE GOD AND HE LOVES ME.
I LEARNED WHO I AM becoming

- Retreatant in Seattle, WA

LOVE WILL BREAK YOU DOWN

Gino Lloyd
Atlanta, GA

I cannot remember the exact date of my first ISP retreat, but I can tell you that when I attended it I was sick and tired of being sick and tired.

I joined the military in Washington, DC. This is where I first picked up hard drugs. I battled with the drugs for over 20 years. Eventually, my brother urged me to move to Atlanta with him, hoping that a geographic change might help me. It was not long after moving to Atlanta that I was back to my active addiction. Eventually I went to Veterans Affairs and tried to start a recovery program but again it was not long until I was back to my addiction and my old ways of living.

When I was 50 years old, I told myself I was going to give recovery another chance. I entered a lock-down program where they spoon-fed me, encouraged me to get a sponsor and to work the 12 steps. This was the last thing I wanted to do, but somewhere along the way something changed. The program began to take hold of me. It began to become a part of my spirit. I began attending Common Ground recovery meetings and eventually Jane Elliott, one of the group leaders, invited me to attend an ISP retreat. On that first retreat, a seed was planted.

The day of the retreat I was filled with apprehension, but the calm I experienced almost immediately was like nothing I have ever experienced. For me, the experience was a reconnection with God and with community. I felt rejuvenated and spiritually connected.

The retreat was not forced. Nothing was forced. Everyone was brilliant and patient and open. I connected deeply with the experience of the

Stations of the Cross. I also truly enjoyed watching the film *Gran Torino*. It was a powerful, powerful movie that prompted a powerful discussion. It showed that when someone loves you, no matter how tough you are, love will break you down and allow you to experience that love fully.

The retreat showed me the wonders God can work in us. When we sit in that circle and one man is talking and he can go into the depths of his soul, do you know how powerful that is? He can talk about anything he wants to between him and God. There is something about sharing, with a group of men, the spiritual aspects of life. The combination of Narcotics Anonymous and the ISP retreat has led to a change in myself right in front of my own eyes.

Eventually, Jane asked me if I was interested in helping to facilitate the retreats. Before experiencing the retreat, I would never have considered a leadership role, but I decided to say yes. I just put one foot in front of the other. Before, I was scared to have such responsibility. Today it helps me. It stretches me and I love that. When I am in the facilitator role I am held more accountable and I love that. I thank God that my life is in order and that I am able to participate in ISP retreats.

LEARNING HOW TO LOVE

Bill Little
Chicago, IL

I'm a recovering alcoholic coming up on three years sober. I grew up in Addison, IL in a very loving family. We ate our meals together, and when I was young we would take nice family vacations, traveling all around the United States. I loved playing hockey. My father would participate with me in sports. He was my best friend and we bowled together for 20 years.

After high school I got a job rebuilding starters in a shop. I held the job for over 18 years. I became foreman and had about 30 people working under me there.

I got married a couple years out of high school but that didn't last too long. She was having an affair and fooling around. We got a divorce and I started drinking a little bit.

Later on, I dated another girl for better than two years, and we were talking about getting married. One day she said she loved me but she didn't need a man in her life. After that she started dating one of my friends and I just gave up, I started drinking real heavy.

Right before that breakup my mother found out she had cancer and passed away. After she died it was just me and my father in the house. He was a diabetic and eventually lost both of his legs and his eyesight. We couldn't afford a live-in nurse or a nursing home so I had to learn how to care for him, to give him his insulin shots and his medications. I had to quit my job and I stayed home with him for five years. He passed away in my arms, just as my mother had.

In the years I was taking care of my father I was drinking pretty big at nighttime. After he passed away, I started working as a mechanic, which I did for a little under ten years. I was drinking too much and I got suspended from work for drinking and I basically didn't care—I just started drinking even more.

I wound up getting drunk one night and falling down some stairs. I was paralyzed and couldn't walk. People had to carry me home. I was drinking so bad I didn't even know what time of day it was. Finally a friend of mine came over to see me and saw the way I was living and my health. He called my neighbor who contacted my sister and told her I was basically lying on my deathbed from drinking. My sister, who I hadn't talked to in seven or eight years, called me and told me to get my rear end to the hospital, which I did. They sent me to a nursing home where I stayed for about a year. It took six or seven months for me to get out of the wheelchair and walk again.

I'd lost my job and had been evicted. At the nursing home they discovered I had arthritis real bad, which meant I wouldn't be able to go back to work. My social security application was denied so I was kicked out of the nursing home. I wound up living for a couple of years at housing programs for the homeless in Chicago.

When I was staying at Pioneer House, a gentleman named Steve talked me into coming on an Ignatian Spirituality Project retreat. It was on the retreat that I learned how to love myself. I also learned how to love other people again. If I didn't care about myself, why should I care about you? Before, I wouldn't give you the shirt off my back. But now, if you need my shirt I'd be the first one to give it to you, because I've got more respect for other people.

After the retreat a lot of people noticed I had this glow over me. I was always smiling and I was looking so forward to the next retreat. The more retreats I went to, the longer this sensation stayed in me. It's a great feeling. I wound up picking myself up and great things are happening to me now since I've been coming to these retreats. There are such wonderful people here and they all love me and I can tell by the way they look. When I greet them at the door, they say, "Billy, I'm so glad to see you."

Since being involved with the ISP retreats, everything seems to be clearer in my head. Small things aren't bothering me anymore; if they are I take a minute to reflect, ask God for guidance and the next thing you know things just happen. I'm learning to take one day at a time. They tell you at AA you'll wind up either in jail, an institution or dead. I went through two of those. I've only got death left and I'm not pressing that issue.

I love being a witness on the retreats, sharing my story. Just the thought of helping somebody, I love it. I needed help myself but I was just too blind to see it. Many times after I speak, men come up and say that what I shared really came home to them. Seeing them again later they've come up to me and said, "I listened to what you told me and I tried it, and that stuff worked!" I'm always looking forward to the next retreat.

It's amazing what God can do. Before coming on the retreats, people had to point out to me how God was in my life but I couldn't see it myself. Since coming on the retreats I can feel God in my life every day. I still need reminders of how God is in my life, but I can see more clearly now that there is a Lord and He's on my side. I'm doing everything I possibly can to keep my life in order. Whenever I get depressed I think about this spiritual program and what it's done for me and it's helping me grow every day. I think about drinking and I think about the things I went through and I don't ever want to go through that again. As long as I stay in contact with God, nothing can hurt me.

HOW MUCH I AM LOVED

Marina Dominguez
Denver, CO

I attended my first ISP retreat in April of 2011. It was several months after my third heart attack in three months' time. I had gone to live in a women's shelter to get off the streets and drugs. I was grateful this agency had a place for women to go and get help to get back on their feet.

At the retreat, my anxieties dissipated instantly with the genuine love and acceptance by the women of ISP. The location was amazing; I felt a sense of peace and tranquility that was so foreign to me. I had never been on a retreat before but it was everything I had needed. It was life changing!

The first thing I remember was how welcome I felt. Walking into the room, I saw a circle of chairs with a beautiful centerpiece in the middle. There were women of all ages gathered there with beautiful inviting smiles on their faces, and arms outstretched for a warm embrace.

The retreat was helpful in a multitude of ways. I feel like I'm still reaping the benefits of that retreat! I would say a lot of the walls I had put up to keep people out came down as a result of that retreat. I'm not saying it was all at once, but gradually, over time, my light shone brighter as my armor came off.

I am a better person because of my continuing relationship with the Ignatian Spirituality Project. I was a woman coming out of a 25-year addiction to alcohol and crack. I had spent ten long, lonely, traumatic years living on the streets of Denver, surviving the best way I knew how… as a prostitute. A lot of baggage came with that lifestyle. I had spent so many years trying to stay away from people. I had it in my mind that if I reject them first they can't reject me.

After that first ISP overnight retreat, I did not go to the follow-up retreat for several reasons, all having to do with my own low self-esteem.

Each month I received a call inviting me to attend the ISP gathering on the third Friday of every month. I eventually gave in and started attending, and I am so grateful that I made that choice. These meetings are still something I look forward to and I have built some incredible friendships with the women of ISP. As I have become more involved with ISP I have become more aware of my own self-worth. I have been transformed!

Now I attend college and I serve as a witness on the retreats. I attended the National Witness Retreat in Pennsylvania, which brought together ISP witnesses from around the country. I have spoken at a few fundraising events. I have an office job on campus that I enjoy tremendously. Would I have all this if I had not gone on that first retreat? I doubt it very much because for the first time in my life I found people who genuinely cared about me and my feelings. I had people that really listened to what I was saying. I began to feel comfortable asking for support and I realized that I had people to pray for me at those times I could not pray for myself.

I give a lot of credit for my continued sobriety to my ISP connections, because feeling connected has always been a big issue for me. I have found calling on my friends from ISP has always been exactly what I needed. The fact that I even feel comfortable in reaching out now is truly a miracle. I am amazed that I have the understanding and presence of mind to know not to succumb to the impulses or urges that occasionally come out of nowhere. I feel the presence of my angels of ISP when I am fighting my inner battles. I feel like I walk with an army now even when I am alone and have feelings of not feeling safe or strong.

I have learned to make a lot of positive changes in my life. Choosing to go to school was the best thing I ever did for myself. I was so emotional walking on campus the first day, just tearing up, wishing my mom was there to see me. I choose who to be friends with and I make sure I don't allow myself to be taken advantage of. I realize now that saying no is okay. I know I can't possibly please everyone, but living my life so that it pleases our Father brings me the most happiness and peace in my life.

I never in my life expected to live to the age of 46. I honestly didn't expect to see 21. I have always struggled with depression and thoughts that the world would be better off without me. I now see those times as God wanting me to get closer to Him and to lean on Him. To the world I am one, but to ONE I am the world!!! I know, now, how much I am loved and I thank ISP for helping me to discover that.

MY HEART EXPANDED WITH LOVE

Kathy Di Fede
San Diego, CA

Even after studying about St. Ignatius, ISP and homelessness to prepare for my role as coordinator of the new San Diego ISP team, I really didn't know what to expect on my first retreat. What surprised me most was what my heart felt about the women experiencing this retreat. It felt as though my heart just expanded with love!

On our second retreat I really connected with one of the women. It was an unexpected and unusual connection. She is much younger than I am and, in fact, attended high school with one of my sons. I felt I had gained a daughter! Her openness in sharing her life and her struggles touched me. Over the course of the weekend I watched her face and eyes change from guarded to trusting. There was hope in her eyes that just continued to grow.

The most difficult part of the ISP retreat is leaving on Sunday. All the love, joy and bonding that happens is just incredible. Each one is a precious jewel, and I have to let them go. I see the hope in all the women, not just those from the shelters but the facilitators also. I hold them all in my heart. I will never forget them.

My new friend, Lisa, is moving on. A new life is opening for her. She has acknowledged God in her life and I believe that the hope will only continue to grow. She said to me that she would like to come back to San Diego as a witness on a future ISP retreat. My hope is that I will see her again and can give her another BIG hug.

Angie Bakely (left)

I KNOW THAT I AM LOVED

Angie Bakely
Detroit, MI

Right from the beginning, I felt unwanted. I am the youngest of 13 children, born to a mother who didn't know she was pregnant for many months and a father who wanted my mother to get an abortion. Obviously, my mother chose not to abort me, but she was overwhelmed with so many children and I grew up feeling unwanted and unloved.

My parents were very strict people. My father was a preacher but he was not loving to his own children. He was mean and abusive and he would not allow me to have friends. I was very unhappy growing up in that house and I started drinking at 17. I couldn't wait to get away from my parents, so at the age of 21 I moved out and got married, but it was a mistake. My husband was violent and abusive to me. When I was seven and a half months pregnant, he stabbed me in the stomach in the middle of the street. The stabbing resulted in my losing my daughter, before she ever had a chance at life, but luckily my son Gabriel survived.

At this point, God helped me save my own life and the life of Gabriel. God gave me the courage to finally leave my husband after being married to him for ten years. But leaving my husband meant that I had no money, so I was on the streets, homeless. I didn't want that for my son, so I gave up custody of him to my brother. It was hard to do, but I knew it was the right thing. I remained homeless for 12 years and my drinking continued. I felt like my life was going around in a vicious, ugly circle and I didn't have anyone to talk to or anyone to care about me. I was filled with anger and I was drinking to make the pain go away, but I realize now that this only made things worse. I was feeling all the pain of the mental and physical abuse I had experienced and I didn't have an outlet to express it so I continued to drink. I smiled to hide the tears that were in my heart and I wouldn't let anyone know the real me. Even I didn't know the real me. At this point, I was someone else and I hated myself, but I just didn't know how to stop.

My turning point was a dream I had about Gabriel. He was calling to me, wanting me to be well and be with him. I know this was God's work. I realized that God didn't bring me this far, just to leave me. He wanted me to find help and to be reunited with Gabriel, so I came to the NOAH Project [a downtown Detroit community center] looking for help. I knew I couldn't drink there and I started going to AA meetings.

Soon after, I was asked if I would like to attend an ISP retreat. I was nervous and anxious about going because I had no idea of what to expect. I thought maybe no one would talk to me. My fears started to go away when I was greeted so kindly and warmly by the facilitators at the door. It didn't take long for me to realize that this retreat was a place where I was able to open up and share my experience with other women without being judged. I didn't feel ashamed to talk about my past, honestly. I could express whatever I wanted, even if it meant crying, and I really liked the feeling of sisterhood that I experienced with the other women. I found that there was another way to deal with my anger, fear and pain without drinking. ISP helped me to understand that I can work through whatever problems I have with God's help.

My life is different now because I feel that I have the power to do whatever I put my mind to. I have also learned that I matter and that I don't need anyone's approval, except my own. The retreat helped me to realize that I am loved and I am beautiful on the inside and on the outside. And I know that God is always with me because he didn't bring me this far just to leave me now.

Since I went on that first ISP retreat people look at me differently. I even walk and talk differently because I have confidence that comes from sobriety and knowing that I am loved. I have enrolled in school and I am working part-time at the NOAH Project. But the best part of my life now is that my son and I have a beautiful relationship and he is proud of me! He tells me all the time how much he loves me and that keeps me on my toes. I want him to always be proud of me.

I am happy and grateful to be able to share my story with other women on the ISP retreats. There is so much peace to be found on the retreats and also a feeling of belonging. By sharing my story and hearing others share theirs, ISP brings a feeling of family to me. I have wanted that feeling of family for my entire life and I have found it with ISP.

GROWING IN GOD'S LOVE

Tina Morrow
Omaha, NE

In April of 2008, I hit my rock bottom, but that lowest point in my life was also the time of my change and renewal. I had been a meth addict for ten years and gradually my life had spiraled out of control. I was estranged from my family, I was breaking the law, I was writing bad checks, stealing from stores and putting my young sons in harm's way by exposing them to the madness of my addiction. I even began making meth and selling it. At first, I loved this life and I was having a ball. Meth made me feel like I was important. I had something everyone wanted, so my house was always full of people and I had control over who could be there. They wanted to be with me and "control" became the key to my addiction.

On April 27, 2008, I was arrested outside of my home and this is when God saved me. I was charged with conspiracy and intent to manufacture meth. The two charges carry a sentence of 25 years to life and 1 to 10 years, to be served in a federal prison. By God's grace, the federal government dropped the conspiracy charge and I pleaded guilty only to the charge of intent to manufacture meth. I was sentenced to one year and one day in prison and I was released in June of 2009.

Prison is not where I wanted to be and I hated it while I was there but it gave me time to find myself. Without this time away from my family and friends and away from meth, I wouldn't be telling you my story. When I was in prison I went on my first retreat. Of course we weren't able to leave the grounds, but it was held on a Saturday and Sunday in one of our class-rooms and it exposed me to the power of God. I can't remember how long we stayed in the classroom, but I do remember it was long enough to feel God's presence and His healing power within me.

After spending that year in prison, I got out and I decided that I was not going to go back to my old life. I wanted to continue to heal myself through God's grace and I jumped at the chance to go to an overnight ISP retreat. I was excited to be there and the first few hours of the retreat were amazing. I met many women with whom I could relate. I felt safe talking about myself and the things I have been through. The love and trust I felt there with all of the women was powerful and energizing.

The scenery of the retreat grounds was beautiful and I remember thanking God for all of His doings. The peace I felt walking the grounds that He had created was incredible. There was a lake on the grounds where I put my feet in the water. I looked up at the sky and thanked Him for letting me feel again. I told God how grateful I was that He had saved me and for allowing me a second chance at living life the way He wanted me to live it. Most importantly, I thanked Him for showing me that I wasn't alone. God showed me that there are many women who have been in my shoes—some much worse than mine—and He put us all in this one place, together, to heal from our wounds.

That first weekend away at the ISP retreat gave me a chance to re-energize, relax, meet other women like myself and take time away from my everyday responsibilities which were causing depression, anxiety and frustration in my life. It brought me closer to God and helped me to remember not to allow worldly pressures to bring me down. I realized that if I keep striving to put God first, then things will go much smoother. I realized that I needed to quit trying to steer the boat by myself and allow God to do it for me.

Another big realization on that retreat was that I can help others by sharing my story. My own story is one of the most powerful gifts God has given me to help others. By sharing my story I can give others hope that sobriety and recovery are possible for them, just like it has been for me. Trusting God and allowing Him to work through me is the key. I have been the witness on many retreats over the last few years and today I am an ISP team member and I help coordinate the retreats here in Omaha.

Besides being a volunteer for ISP, I instruct a class called "Celebrate Recovery" at Restored Hope, which is a transitional living program for single moms who are homeless, who have suffered from domestic abuse or who have an addiction and want to get back on track. I am also a mom of three boys. They are my motivation for continuing in my recovery and sobriety and I love them more than life itself. God has blessed me with all three of them and he continues to give me the strength to be a good mother to each one of them.

From the first day of my first retreat I have been growing in God's love and trusting my life to Him. I am now in the process of purchasing a home for myself and my boys, I drive a safe, comfortable car, I have true friendships, I have a job I love and I continue to grow in my faith. I am living today with no regrets and with the forgiveness and the love of Jesus. It's been a most incredible journey and as I look back and see how far God has brought me, I am grateful beyond words.

GOD

14. What did you learn about yourself?

That god loves me, when I didn't feel that before I came. I learned about myself that Im more patient then what I thought. And I can take in things and just relax.

- Retreatant in Morristown, NJ

15. How did this retreat impact your spiritual/recovery journey?

It made me Realize that I am loved By God & that through God's Grace I am here For a purpose

- Retreatant in West Palm Beach, FL

GIVING MY HEART TO GOD

Stephen Hopkins
Washington, DC

I grew up in the Anacostia area of southeast Washington, DC. Coming up, I made some choices in life that sent me down the wrong path. In that spiral going down, I got involved with drugs, and a whole lot of other things that just led me to more drugs. My life was chaos. I've been shot three times, I've been stabbed, and that still didn't get my attention to stop using. I continued to use more. I was in and out of prison, I would come home and I would still use. I was on parole and I would still use. Just take the consequences, send me back to jail, that was my attitude. All my life everything I'd done was about self-destruction.

It took me a long time to finally say that I needed to change. I came home from prison the last time, and I had made up my mind this was it. I had lost everything, so when I came home I had nothing to come home to. I got involved with a drug program in the penitentiary, going to NA meetings, spiritual groups. I wanted to continue that, so I went into a transitional program to continue my sobriety and move on in my life. That really helped me because my thirst for change was there, but I needed a lot more as far as my spirituality part.

The program sent me to an ISP retreat, my first retreat in my lifetime, at the age of 56. When I went on the retreat, I didn't know what to expect, so I asked my case manager and he just told me to have an open mind. That's how I carried it. The retreat experience was about serenity. It was so peaceful there, which was something I really needed. The peace and quiet gave me time to think of where I'm at and what I need to do with myself.

The guidance I got through learning to listen to other people, not trying to do it my way, it helped me with all of that. The retreat opened my eyes up to show me that I was right where God wanted me to be.

I came to realize that the presence of God in my life meant a lot more today than in the past. The only time I would grab God was when I was in trouble—"Oh, God, get me out of this." Now I grab hold of God to take all of that off my shoulders. When I can't carry it with me, I give it to God and let go. I've learned that through these last four or five years now. I don't even think about the drugs, my lifestyle is changing.

The retreat was so great for me that I knew I had to share it. I got my friend Reggie involved with it, so he could have that same experience, and he's been on board ever since. That's a grace for me, to see another person that came from my walk giving God his time.

When I was first part of the ISP team, they would give me things to do on the retreat. I had a group to lead or something. At first I was afraid, but then I realized that I was in God's house. There's no wrong in how I do this. He's going to lead me in the right way. That gave me confidence in speaking to guys, and taking on my responsibilities. I want to give back. This is my way of giving back. I just ask for God to lead me. I take a couple of deep breaths, relax, and I let it flow. I let God lead. I don't drive anymore, I let God do all the driving.

Today I live a lot better than I used to live. I have my own place, I go to ISP spiritual groups, I spend time with my family. I've learned to give back to God, to give God some time out of the day, to talk to God in my own way. My addiction has made me who I am today. I'm a person trying to have a better relationship with God.

My mother got sick recently and I got in my feelings about that. I had to remember who the architect of this is. He knows best what needs to be done. My selfishness had to get out of the way. I asked for some prayers with the guys in my spiritual group at ISP. And I came to realize that God gave me the key to love, the key to love is my heart. I had to go into my heart and give it to God.

When you look on the face of man, you look on the face of God. I want to treat people in that Godly fashion. I look at the Godliness in every person because I want them to see it in me. No matter how much chaos and negativity is in a person, I'm going to recognize the God in them and show them the God in me.

ALL ABOUT GOD

Jonathan Irving
Akron, OH

Jonathan Irving successfully graduated from the Salvation Army program in Akron three times, but the first two times he "conned" his way through the program. It was only the last time, after attending an ISP retreat, that he truly found out "all about God."

Jonathan was born in Montgomery, Alabama, moved to Cleveland, and later Akron. He fell into a lifestyle of abusing drugs and alcohol, and for a time made his living as a pimp. Jonathan entered the Salvation Army residential program in Akron three times, but the first two times, after completing the program, he went back to his former life. The third time he was there, he was advised by the man and wife team running the shelter that he should go on an ISP retreat. He did, and after he came back, he said that he went to his room, put the Big Book and the Bible on top of his locker, fell to his knees before them, and started to pray. He said that the room was spinning around and "lit up" and he couldn't stop crying. When he finally rose to his feet, he said his desire for drugs was gone.

Jonathan later became a witness for ISP, and today is a valued member of the ISP men's team in Akron. Finding God, Jonathan says, does not take away your troubles, but it enables you to deal with them without drugs and alcohol. He gives the example of his son Brandon being in jail, and how concerned he is about that. However, today he prays about it and does not manage his pain and anxiety with substance abuse.

Jonathan now lives with his brother and studies at the University of Akron. He related a story of being in a class with his son, Courtland.

Because Courtland referred to him as "Dad" and students did not know of their relationship, they assumed his nickname was "Dad" and also began to call him that. Jonathan assured them that he was "Dad" only to Courtland, and "Jonathan" to the rest.

As Jonathan says, his troubles and concerns have not vanished, but as long as he keeps it "all about God" he is fine.

THE DESIRE FOR GOD

Tom Baldonado
Denver, CO

It was always an awkward moment for me, waiting for the light to turn green at any of our city intersections. Inevitably there they'd be, someone standing on the corner or walking up and down the street median with a tattered cardboard sign, "Anything Helps. God Bless." Not wanting to make eye contact I pretended to be busy in my car, hoping the light would quickly change. It never really felt good to me and it began to nag at me so eventually I began to carry a stack of one dollar bills in the console of my car. Easy enough, just roll down the window and hand them a dollar bill. The street corner beggars were always gracious and thankful and it made me feel pretty good. They seemed to be happy about my donation and I finally could quit feeling guilty about trying to avoid them at each traffic stop.

At a class I was attending on Ignatian Spirituality, a gentleman began to talk about the Ignatian Spirituality Project. He asked, "Do you ever wonder what you should do when you are approached by people asking for your spare change?" I figured I had that answer down pat but as he explained, "If you really want to give a true gift, I invite you to find out about the retreats we put on for men and women experiencing homelessness." My initial thought was that I couldn't imagine what those would be like. Spend a weekend with them? Handing out a dollar bill and continuing along my way seemed to be working pretty well for me. He continued on to explain that what ISP gave was so much more than pocket change. They provided a comfortable place, food and peaceful time for people to discover or reignite a relationship with their Higher Power, Creator, God. The ISP retreats are an opportunity to give people a gift that will never run out and never go dry. Truly, this stopped me right in my tracks and made a very strong impression on me. I continued on my way with my street corner donations but a seed had been planted and I began to wonder what it would be like to be part of something bigger, everlasting and deeper than I was presently giving.

As I continued to deepen my own experience of Ignatian Spirituality I began to see a spiritual director. After hearing of my interest in ISP, he introduced me to the coordinator of the local men's retreats. Before I knew it I was attending the next ISP men's retreat. It was nothing like I thought it would be. When I saw the desire for God that the men at the retreat had come with I was sold. I truly wanted to become part of something more than a handout. I wanted God to use me to give something bigger, His hope and His love.

Three and a half years later, I'm now the local men's coordinator. All I can say is be careful what you ask for when you place your desires into God's hands. Oh yes, there are many moments of thinking I don't know what I'm doing and how are things possibly going to come together. But once I catch my breath I just say, "Hey God, this is Yours. I'll do all I can but this is Your project, not mine." I'm continually amazed at how God always sends strong team members and retreatants every time. ISP is truly God's project and I couldn't be more fulfilled, happy and excited to be part of His plan to provide everlasting food and drink.

GOD COMES TO ME

Amanda (right) with Linda
Catanzaro, Coordinator of the
Cleveland ISP Women's Team.

Amanda
Cleveland, OH

Amanda began attending the ISP Spiritual Recovery Group at the Edna House for Women in Cleveland when she returned there for support following a relapse. The Edna House is dedicated to providing means and opportunity to women affected by alcohol and drug addiction to achieve sobriety. They work on developing mentally, spiritually and emotionally through a blend of 12-step recovery, life and career training, volunteerism and therapeutic interventions. Through attending our spiritual recovery group, Amanda learned about our ISP retreats. She attended a Day of Reflection in January followed by our overnight retreat in the spring and follow-up gathering in May. During this time, she continued to attend the Spiritual Recovery Group.

Our women's ISP team has been privileged to witness Amanda's spiritual transformation over the many months we have gotten to know her and hear her story. She served as a witness on our fall retreat this year and her sharing was inspiring and powerful. She completed Phase II at Edna House and began to incorporate some of the recovery principles she had been learning into her daily life. Amanda was provided job skills training and eventually secured a job. She was also reunited with her husband and son. Throughout this period her spiritual transformation continued. Her relationship with God became the guiding force in her life and continues to sustain her recovery.

Amanda gave a witness talk at our second annual benefit in November. She spoke very movingly about the impact of the ISP retreats and the spiritual recovery group on her spiritual journey and about the resultant transformation that she has experienced. She ended her witness with a powerful quotation from a reflection that she had written while on an overnight retreat. It expresses her story of hope and transformation:

God comes to me when I am in pain. And bestows me with healing...
God comes to me when I am distracted and re-centers my focus...
God comes to me when I feel the world has lost its color and gives me rose-colored lenses...
God comes to me in the storms of my life to calm it, or let it rage and to calm me...

ENCOUNTERING GOD IN NEW WAYS

Ann Rotermund
St. Louis, MO

Having led the ISP team in St. Louis for several years, I've had the priv-ilege to participate in many retreats, where I encounter God in ever new and different ways. To give just one example, on one of our retreats we broke off into pairs for an exercise entitled, "Who is God to Me?" I was paired with a very young woman. We each had a piece of paper, and could write or draw our personal image of God, whatever that may be. When we settled ourselves I noticed that her paper was untouched by ink. I asked about it and she replied, "I don't think I have ever had an experience of God." I found her answer distressingly honest and immediately asked the Holy Spirit to direct me.

It was a beautiful spring day. We walked out in the courtyard of the retreat center. All manner of flowers were in bloom. I invited her to touch, smell and visually experience this life. She quietly and reverently moved along using her senses and was very present to each plant. She then said to me, "Why am I doing this?" I answered, "You are having an experience of a creating God." To which she replied, "Now I know what you mean by an experience of God."

LIVING OUT GOD'S CALLING

Yvonne Velasco
Orange County, CA

My name is Yvonne and I am a guest at Isaiah House of Orange County, California [a Catholic Worker house of hospitality]. In February of 2015, I came to Isaiah House after having lost my job and home.

As you might imagine, I was a little displaced when the opportunity to attend an Ignatian Spirituality Project retreat came along a few weeks after arriving at Isaiah House. At the time, though, there was a sincere desire in me to make a change in my life. There was a feeling like when something is broken and you don't know how it broke or how to fix it. I hoped that the retreat might give me the opportunity to really look into myself and finally feel whole again.

As we drove to Oceanside, I was literally bursting at the seams with things to get off my chest and wounds to heal in my life. I thank God that I had the chance to go. It was at this retreat that, not only the healing I needed began, but also a seed was planted. I now am working for a large healthcare provider and am saving money to move out. I should be ready in about three months. Mostly, I now know that it's not enough to just work and pay for a place to live and run after the American Dream... but it is more important to realize and live out God's calling in your life. I see now that the Lord allowed me to go through the things that I have so that I can help others in the same situation. As I write this, my biggest goal is to begin working on a degree in theology next year. I plan to become a chaplain one day and see to the needs of the poor and the broken, the hurting, the destitute... people like me. I am as broken as any person sleeping on a sidewalk.

Thank you for providing these retreats for us. Thank you for loving the broken.

DEEPENING MY RELATIONSHIP WITH GOD

Issac Sneed
Boston, MA

I grew up with both parents and seven siblings in a Boston housing project. Father was a vicious alcoholic, physically abusing everyone including Mother. There was no spirituality in the home, though a Bible was present. I was an honor student in school but dropped out in the ninth grade. Got involved in drinking, marijuana and hustling. But God saved me from myself even at that time. I thought a good job would make me feel better about myself. I heard the recruitment for Boston Police so I applied and completed the academy. But my self-seeking values continued.

In five years I was arrested for passing forged Percocet prescriptions and received a suspended sentence. Shame and self-loathing fueled my addiction. I continued to drink and use during the next ten years, bouncing through rehab programs. In ten years, I was in rehab again. Coming to, I felt dirty and went to take a shower. I passed a mirror and my life flashed before me. It scared me. I fell to my knees, cried and begged for help. The weight was lifted.

I went to a residential program, completed it and was hired on staff. I was promoted several times, landing as the program director with only a GED. I stayed clean ten years and my life came back together. Humility left and pride and ego were back. I failed to enlarge my spiritual life. I took some painkillers for ruptured discs and relapsed. Using again, I tore down all I had gained, especially my self-worth. So I ran away. I went to New York and languished there for ten years.

I met a Godly man who was in recovery while I was in in the hospital in New York. I was homeless and had conned my way into a bed, feigning illness. This man was jaundiced. I overheard the doctor tell him to basically get his affairs in order. A death sentence. But that man turned to me and shared a message that reignited my spirit. He gave me the fare to return to Boston. Everything clicked again. I got clean in the shelter, attended my first ISP retreat and I have stayed involved since.

ISP helps me to deepen my relationship with God, the same God that was with me all the time. I moved into my own place and assist ISP by using my previous experience in connecting with new retreatants. We use all of God's tools to enlighten them. We are truly our brothers' keeper!

The message I received early in life was self-reliance. I spent a lot of time learning that self-reliance was of no use to me when it came to addiction. Once I was able to become honest with myself about that, I became open to the possibility of help. I saw that help was there all the time. It saved me from myself, addiction and got me out of New York to the shelter.

ISP was introduced to me as a spiritual program. It enhanced my recovery program and I use it in conjunction with my recovery. I was glad that there was no preaching. It gave me the opportunity to choose for myself. As I met the Jesuits they directed me and taught me about St. Ignatius in a way I could incorporate the exercises in my life. No pressure. Willingness. I use the same outreach with others. A large part of it is modeling after what was given to me in such a way that it's practical. Being able to share, teach and model what I've been shown is the best way for me to carry a message to newer individuals pursuing spirituality through ISP.

COMMUNITY

16. What did you like best about this retreat? The Bond I feel with GOD and the other men in The retreat.

- Retreatant in St. Louis, MO

16. What did you like best about this retreat?

Friendship

- Retreatant in Baltimore, MD

I'M NOT ALONE

Danny Prowell
St. Louis, MO

I grew up in St. Louis, right downtown in the projects. Living in the projects, in the inner city, bad is good. The people I looked up to were dope dealers, pimps, people like that. This is all I knew. I started getting incarcerated early. I got my first case when I was 12 years old, and it's been like that the majority of my life. I left home at 15. I've been a hustler all my life. I started using alcohol and drugs to mask my hurt. Basically it was peer pressure. I started off smoking weed, drinking beer, moving on up to the real drugs. By the time I was 16, I was messing with cocaine, trying anything. I didn't have a particular drug of choice, I just liked to get high.

The majority of my adult life I've been locked up in different institutions. In 1989 they gave me a mandatory sentence of 15 years. When I got out in 2004, they introduced me to crack and that's when my journey really started. That's when the nightmare started, the homelessness, the messed-up part. A lot of my friends were dead and a lot were incarcerated, so I basically was out here by myself. I was out here doing whatever, supporting my habit, and looking for a way out, but I couldn't find a way out.

I called my aunt and she told me to come to Detroit, they might be able to help me out there. I went to Detroit and stayed clean for six months. I got a job up there, one of the first real jobs I had, at a funeral home. It was cool, I was making $550 a week. Now I'm walking around with all this money and I didn't go to a treatment center because I thought I could do it on my own. So of course I relapsed. I was still working, hiding my addiction, and it was all bad. I woke up one day in a hotel room with some women, I don't even know who these women were. I was in the bathroom when I came to myself with a pipe in one hand and about ten stones in the other. That's when the clarity hit me, like, "What am I doing?" I left everything, I left the pipe, I left the drugs. I got on the bus and I don't know why I got on this bus. I must have been looking so horrible that the bus driver didn't even ask for bus fare. He said, "You sick, son?" I don't even remember what I said. He told me, "Sit here" and the bus took off. It stopped at this hospital. He told me, "Son, go up there to the sixth floor and tell those people you need help."

I went up there and I remember them doing paperwork, processing me. I slept most of the time. They put me in a van and took me to this treatment center called Sobriety House. I was there for nine months. That's when I started really getting it together. They taught me up there, it's not the drugs that made you do what you do, it's your behavior. They deal with core issues up there. They explained to me that I had to change the way I think—if you think about using again, talk to somebody. It worked! I learned to recognize my thoughts, when I thought about using, and say, that's bad, I can't do that.

I got a job in Detroit in a hospital. One day my mom called and told me she was sick with cancer. This was in 2010. She had had cancer for a couple of years but hadn't told me because she didn't want me back down in St. Louis. I came down and she was in hospice—I got to spend six or seven months with her. So she saw me clean.

My mom died, I was back in St. Louis and what was I going to do? I was putting in applications for a job and stuff like that and I just happened to be passing by the St. Patrick Center. Somebody told me they help you find jobs. I went there, and they also had alcohol and drug education classes, which I felt like I still needed. I started going, but I was really depressed, with my mom having just died. The St. Patrick Center was a safe haven for me. I started participating in the classes, talking to the counsellors, taking meditation classes. I calmed down. I used to be a mess—I was really depressed, wanting to use, but knowing using was bad for me.

I started feeling—you know a lot of people on drugs have no feelings. I would talk to Miss Ann [Rotermund], and I would cry and she became like my mother. I started taking her suggestions, like getting back in school.

Miss Ann saw that I was trying, that I was participating in all the programs, and she asked me to come on the ISP retreat. Saturday morning she picked us up and we went to the retreat house. I was looking at this place, and I remembered being over here years ago. I looked out a window and the house across the street was the house where I took my first hit of crack when I got out of the penitentiary. Right across the street, on the corner, was the house where I started getting high. I just started crying. Miss Ann asked what was wrong and I told her. God had taken me full circle. It was seven years later. That blew my mind. I knew God was working. God sure moves in mysterious ways.

The retreat was wonderful, you feel the peace when you walk in. You get to bond with different guys from different places, you get to talk to people from all walks of life. One guy was an architect, one was a dentist. A lot of us [retreatants] asked, why are y'all [facilitators] talking to us, why are y'all here? What's the motive? Why do you want to talk to me? Then those guys are open, and they got their own issues! [When you're homeless] you're walking around these streets and people don't speak to you. They look at you like you're a can on the street. Somebody talking to you, that's a big thing. Your self-esteem is so low, you feel like you're nothing. When people show you that you are a person, and they tell you their own problems, it opens things up. It's not a black and white thing, or a rich and poor thing, it's a "you" thing, do "you" want to do better? You've got to humble yourself, you can't do it alone.

The retreat had a profound effect. It was a beautiful experience. It opened some doors up. It let me know that everybody, not just street people, has issues, the world has issues. After being out there, sleeping in cardboard boxes, sleeping in vacant houses, in this place they got a bed for you, they're showing you that you're a decent human being. The groups are superb, they're real personal with good sharing. I really loved it. I bonded with some guys. These guys were thinking just like I was thinking. That was the beautiful thing about it—I'm not alone. That's what the retreat shows you, you're not alone

I understand miracles today and I understand blessings. Today I've got a wife, a brand new car, a home. I'm not perfect, I've still got character defects, but I'm not using, I'm not stealing, I'm not selling drugs, I go to church every Sunday, I'm just a happy person now. My wife has never been in trouble. She's a Christian. She's never been to jail. To me that was a miracle, that a woman like that would like somebody like me. I wake up every morning and thank God for her. She really teaches me to feel. Like I said, for 50 years I had no feelings. I would take your wallet, take your shoes, I would take you, with no problem. I'm different now, I have compassion for people.

At the retreat, I felt a feeling of satisfaction, a feeling of purpose, that God wanted me to do something, that He had a plan for me. Now I come to the St. Patrick Center and I facilitate classes. I come on the ISP retreats and share my story. Volunteering keeps me busy. I kind of hate that I had to get into my fifties to find this, but this is where God wanted me at this particular time in my life.

A FEELING OF BELONGING

Dave·C.
Portland, OR

My name is Dave. I'm in recovery from a life of distrust and self-will. I have been seeking answers for over 20 years, and within this journey God's spark has grown ever brighter in me. I've been told many times, "the greatest distance I will ever travel is across that space between my head and my heart." I've learned the true depth of my brokenness, but it wasn't until I began to open my heart that I could feel hope.

I was well aware of what it was like to participate in a process group of peers. I had also begun to seek God at a greater depth, yet I was still trying to think my way through. My first opportunity to become involved with an ISP retreat came in spring 2014. I didn't know much about it but I was aware of the spiritual focus. Yes, I thought this could be an open door for God. Although apprehensive, I was excited at the chance to feel God at a deeper level.

The first thing we did at the retreat was a bit like what I thought a family gathering might start out like when "coming home for a holiday." I felt a belonging. As the weekend progressed and I gradually stepped out of my apprehension into the spirit of the moment, a view of the real value of relationships crept in. I began to feel something I had only thought about in other group settings. I found the opportunity and willingness to step beyond some of my self-imposed boundaries. I went home with a deeper sense of my own worth and a new openness towards others and Christ.

In the fall of that same year I was invited to attend a second ISP retreat, this time as the witness. Seeing this as an opening to grow in Christ while giving back, I went with a plan and recorded my thoughts on paper. When the time to share my story came that same feeling of His Spirit being with us filled me. As I shared, what He put in my heart began to flow through. My notes quickly became unnecessary. The result for both myself and the other men was a closeness that stayed with us throughout our retreat.

Although I was seeking a kind of relational awakening, I believe that these retreats create an atmosphere of openness where God's spirit becomes unmistakable. I have gained insights through both of these retreats that years of structured interaction hadn't allowed me to open up to.

I walked into my first retreat with a focus on what I hoped to find, but I encountered something much more. And again as the witness, I left with more than what I brought. I can honestly say from the heart that these experiences have been both a gift and a blessing. As I write this story that feeling of renewal comes back large. I believe that wherever you are in your life's journey, these retreats are a heart-opening place to pause.

A SHARED JOURNEY

Karen Clifton
Washington, DC

We are all broken and it is through God's mercy, experienced through community, that we are restored. ISP is labeled as retreats for those who have experienced homelessness and are addressing their addictions. But haven't we all experienced homelessness of one kind or another? If our addiction is not alcohol or drugs, what is it?

The retreats are transformative for all of us who are privileged to attend. What a gift to be in a prayerful environment and have the opportunity to remember God's presence and abundance. During the course of the retreat, we move onto holy ground. We are witnesses to one another, we share in our vulnerability, we name our fears.

ISP retreats are not an "us and them" experience; they are a shared journey. They are a healing journey for all who allow themselves to travel inward, to name their fears, to acknowledge their participation in bad choices, to recognize God's presence throughout their whole lives, to ask for God's forgiveness and healing, to begin being restored to their communities. Through this flow within the retreat we recognize the vastness of God's mercy and the power of prayer.

We hear and read the stories of how people are transformed through attending the ISP retreat. What about the privileged facilitating teams who have the opportunity to attend? We also are walking testimonies to God's continuing creative work and endless mercy.

THE MOST DIRECT
ROAD TO GOD

Jay Burke
Boston, MA

I recently read a Jesuit's comment on prayer. It went something like, "I began to pray out of obligation and now I pray out of need." That holds true for me and ISP as well: "I began ISP out of obligation and now I volunteer out of need."

During my two years as coordinator of Boston's ISP team, I have experienced the love of God more frequently and more deeply than in all my 63 years beforehand. Since I neither have the time nor the memory to list all the graces I've received over those two years, I'll simply share some from the past two weeks.

The week of Thanksgiving brought a special reunion with one of my close homeless friends. Estranged from his 17-year-old daughter for ten years before attending an ISP retreat, he reconciled with her following the retreat. She ended up coming to town for Thanksgiving week. They spent time getting reacquainted with each other and with his family. Thank you God and ISP.

That same week I was sharing some of the stresses and worries in my own life with my spiritual reflector, who supports me in my ISP work. Through his reflection, I was able to sit with my discomfort and not let it paralyze me. I was able to see more clearly some attachments that were unnecessarily burdening me. As a result, I was able to act with more freedom in this stressful situation than I had known in the past. Thank you God and ISP.

This past Friday I met with ten men experiencing homelessness at one of our weekly Spiritual Tune-Up gatherings. As we recite in the opening blessing,

We gather together in honor and respect for the dignity of each one of us:

- to have time apart from our busy lives,
- to remind ourselves of God's unconditional love,
- to reconnect with our love for one another and
- to recommit to being open to this love from God, from each other, and from ourselves.
- In gratitude and hope we meet, we share, and we pray.

In *The Jesuit Guide to (Almost) Everything*, James Martin, SJ quotes Sister Helen Prejean (author of *Dead Man Walking*): "The most direct road that I have found to God is in the faces of poor and struggling people." For me, the most direct road to God is in the faces of my homeless ISP friends, especially around the circle at our weekly Spiritual Tune-Up gatherings. Their authentic humility, mutual love, and radical faith in God humble and inspire me. Thank you God and ISP.

These are just a few of several ISP experiences over the past two weeks. And they only scratch the surface. My daily prayer has increased thanks to ISP. My personal faith has deepened. I experience the fruits of hope and peace and joy more frequently than ever before. As one of my homeless friends shared at Friday's Spiritual Tune-Up, "I hope I'm going to Heaven. Actually, I feel like I'm in Heaven right now." Thank you God and thank you ISP.

Like many of our volunteers around the country, Jay Burke serves with the Ignatian Volunteer Corps.

HEALING

What did you learn about yourself?

I'm a child of God, which he has forgiven me, He loves me.

— Retreatant in Louisville, KY

What did you learn about yourself?

I learned to trust more. I learned to open up and share
I learned to take my time with healing and my recovery
I learned to be proud of who I am

— Retreatant in Victoria, BC

GOD'S LOVE AND HEALING

Tom Wendt
Omaha, NE

My life has been one "God thing" after another. That is the only way to explain how and why I am alive today and able to tell my story.

I was raised in Owensboro, Kentucky in a rigidly Catholic family. I was a big kid who loved sports and I ended up playing basketball for a college in Louisiana. Before college, I rarely drank alcohol, but college life was different. Everyone I knew drank and I started drinking then as well. Soon I met my future wife, fell in love, got married and eventually had four kids. I took a job as a welding inspector and continued drinking daily. It put a huge strain on my marriage and eventually my wife left with three of our kids. Our oldest, Brittany, who was 12, stayed with me for four years. It was after she left and went back to Louisiana to live with her mother that the tragedies began and my life began to spiral out of control. Two more marriages failed with two more children. I was blaming God for each one of the tragedies and I was angry.

The first tragedy was losing my brother to suicide. We had always been close and I never saw it coming. I was angry at God for taking my brother from me. Next came one of the worst tragedies that I could ever imagine. My beautiful daughter Brittany died in an automobile accident at the age of 20. If I thought I was angry at God before, my anger now exploded. Then, my oldest son was severely burned over 60% of his body in a paper mill explosion. God was out to get me and my family. After that, my mother died and within one year, my father died as well.

The tragedies that I had experienced, and my anger at God, pushed me from an alcohol addiction into a meth addiction and eventually I was arrested. I was facing federal charges which could earn me 100 years in prison and $12 million in fines. It felt like a death sentence to me and at that point in my life I didn't care if I lived or died. I had pushed all of my family and friends away and I felt completely hopeless.

After detox, I ended up at Sienna Francis House in "The Miracles Treatment Program" and I started going to AA meetings. It's much easier to work the program if you have a Higher Power but I had so much anger with God that I didn't think I could do it. One day I was at a meeting and I heard a guy talking about God. I told the guy after the meeting that I didn't think I could do this AA thing because God and I have an arrangement— "I don't ask Him for anything and he doesn't give me anything. He just takes." The guy said, "You've got this program licked then, because good or bad, you've already got a relationship with God." It made me stop and think.

On Brittany's birthday, I woke up so angry at God I knew I had to tell someone about it. I walked to Catholic Charities, looking for a priest to talk to, but there was none to be found. I went to the Jesuit offices at Creighton University but I was told I would have to make an appointment and come back another time. I even tried to go to confession at a local Catholic church, just to find a priest to talk to. I waited in line and when I finally got to the front, the door opened and the priest came out. He had to end the confessions because it was time for him to start Mass. Once again, I felt God didn't care about me and I was angrier than ever. I decided to stay for Mass. When the priest started his homily and said, "Today, I want to talk to everybody about being angry at God," the hairs on the back of my neck stood up.

The next day, I met with the priest and told him all the reasons I was angry with God. It was a turning point just to be able to vocalize all my feelings and hear the priest tell me that it was okay to feel that way. I ended up thanking God for the 20 years of life I had with my daughter and I began to accept my brother's suicide a bit better. This was the first of many "God things."

I was still in The Miracles Treatment Program awaiting my trial when Bill Keck, the founder, and Linda Albrecht, my counselor, told me that I would be going on an ISP retreat over the weekend. The first thing I noticed, besides the serenity of the place, were the facilitators. It was hard to believe that these guys were giving their own free time to be with addicts like me. They were so close to God and they were getting nothing for themselves. I had a huge amount of admiration and respect for them and I enjoyed the retreat. It was a definite "God thing."

I was asked to give my witness on the next ISP retreat—another "God thing" because why would anyone want to hear my story? My anger at God was becoming less and less and I had been taught at AA to give back because God has given so freely to me, so I went and told my story. Once again, I had a powerful experience of God's love and healing. Now I am an ISP team member and the witness on the men's retreats. Each retreat gives me strength to stay in my recovery and connect with the men and with God.

After more than two years of delays, my trial finally came before a judge. I was nervous because of the amount of time that I was facing but I was ready for my sentence. I was shocked when I got to the courthouse and saw about 20 of my friends and acquaintances there to support me—another "God thing." I was even more shocked when I heard the judge waive any prison time and sentence me to only five years of supervised probation—the biggest "God thing" ever!

I just celebrated five years in recovery—a "God thing"—and I have a good job and a house on the west side of town—more "God things." After many years of being estranged from my children, I enjoy a great relationship with them now—continual "God things."

A few months ago, I was offered the job of a lifetime, but it meant that I would have to move to Baltimore. After praying about it, I decided to stay right here in Omaha with ISP, my AA program and all my friends and family who help to keep me sober. No amount of money or prestige can replace all the "God things" that have gotten me to this place. I am grateful for each and every one of them.

MY OWN WOUNDS COULD
BE HEALED

Erwin Jugarap
San Francisco, CA

Erwin Jugarap suffered a violent childhood, but experienced healing on an ISP retreat that continues to unfold in his life. On retreat he was able to share his story. As a child, his father's regular beatings had turned him towards a life of violence from an early age. In middle school he joined a gang and would frequently get in fights with rival gang members. This led to suspensions and to further beatings at home. A few years later Erwin dropped out of high school and became addicted to alcohol. His gang lifestyle, addictive behavior and violent ways led to incarceration several times during his twenties. He felt that the root of his violence was the abuse he experienced from his father. Though his father experienced a religious conversion late in life, he died without expressing his love and forgiveness of Erwin. Erwin, in turn, had not expressed forgiveness of his father.

After the story sharing there was a 15-minute break. Erwin was agitated by the feelings that were stirred by telling his story so he decided to go for a walk. Something drew him to walk a path at the retreat center that was lined with metal plaques of the Stations of the Cross. As he passed each plaque he found himself becoming calmer. Finally, he came to the plaque that showed Jesus taken down from the cross and held by his mother. Erwin was drawn to the wounds of Jesus and found himself spontaneously reaching out his hand to touch the wounds. A profound and mysterious experience began to unfold with that simple gesture. When he touched the metal plaque he felt metal on his chest. He touched his chest and discovered he was wearing his Dad's metal necklace with his Dad's ring attached to it, a gift his mother had given him after his father's death. "I became silent inside and heard a voice," he said. "I knew it was my father's voice telling me that he forgave me. In that moment I felt free of my past. I felt hope. In touching the wounds of Jesus, I knew that my own wounds could be healed." He began to feel love for his father warming his heart. He was able truly to forgive him for all the violence and abuse he had suffered growing up.

When he returned to the group after the break Erwin appeared transformed. His physical agitation and the edge of anger and resentment in his voice were gone. He appeared relaxed and free, full of joy, hope and bewildered wonder. As he struggled to put into words the deep healing that had just occurred, it was clear that he was speaking from the depths of his heart.

In the months following the retreat Erwin's heart continued to open. The words of Gospel songs now made sense to him because he was experiencing what the words described. He found himself volunteering at a drop-in center for the homeless, cutting their hair and tending to their needs. "I never would have paid attention to those kinds of people before," he said. At the graduation ceremony for his recovery program Erwin was recognized for exceptional volunteer work with people in the program—driving others to appointments, taking on the responsibilities of house manager and many other acts of service.

Erwin views the moment when he touched the wounds of Christ and felt his own wounds healed as the key turning point in his recovery, a moment when he truly surrendered to God as his Higher Power. That moment continues to be a source of strength and encouragement as he continues his recovery and rebuilds his life.

THE TURNING POINT IN MY RECOVERY

Creshawn Smith
Cleveland, OH

At 18 years old Creshawn Smith was a high school dropout and addict who had lost everything—his family, his home, and his hope for the future. "I was heading down the wrong path, not doing what you're supposed to be doing, and doing everything you're not supposed to do," says Creshawn.

Creshawn, who repeated ninth grade three times, was just starting tenth grade when he burned his last bridge. "My grandmother had enough. My mother had enough. My auntie had enough. They each put me out, and I ran out of places to go." Creshawn ended up homeless, living and sleeping in a city park for six weeks. "I didn't care what happened to me. I knew I wouldn't amount to anything and things would never get better."

One morning Creshawn was awakened by a guardian angel of sorts, a park ranger, who found him sleeping on a bench. She cared enough to find out his story. Instead of arresting him, she gave him bus fare and meal money from her own pocket and directed him to 2100 Lakeside, an emergency shelter in downtown Cleveland. Creshawn began the slow, painful process of recovery there and then moved into Y Haven, which offers transitional housing for homeless men suffering from addiction.

While at Y Haven, Creshawn was invited to attend an ISP retreat. When he first introduced himself on the retreat, he was so bashful he could barely whisper his name. "I can't talk in front of people," he said in a halting, barely audible voice. But in small groups he slowly found the confidence to share about himself. Before the retreat, he wasn't sure he wanted to stick with his recovery. But afterwards, he found the willingness "to do anything to stay sober" and saw the possibility that his life "could get better and better."

Creshawn describes the ISP retreat as "remarkable, life-changing, and the turning point in my recovery." It was a quiet place to get away and be peaceful and serene. But more than that, it was a safe place to be with guys "just like me" who were not afraid to say anything.

The most moving part of the retreat was the hand cleansing and healing service in the Chapel. "I was overcome with a sudden urge to pray," and left feeling "like a new man."

Creshawn became a regular at Cleveland's monthly post-retreat "First Friday" meetings. "Refresher courses," he says, "to connect with my Higher Power and talk about things going on in my life." Creshawn has also been reunited with his own family, the same ones who had given up on him. Today Creshawn sees himself as an "energetic, outgoing, young man who likes to have clean, sober fun."

Creshawn stuck around long enough for the miracle to happen. He went back to school for his GED. He was accepted into a Public Works project through the Center for Job and Family Services. He will spend a year or more living on a campus in Cincinnati to learn a trade and become certified as an automotive technician, where he will spend as much time with computer systems as with a wrench.

Creshawn also became involved in a play at the Cleveland Public Theater as part of its outreach program. He played the prodigal son, the central role in a play loosely based on the lives of Creshawn and 12 other men from his transitional housing facility. He later returned to the Cleveland Public Theater, where he was invited to do a poetry reading with members of the world-renowned Cleveland Orchestra. He confidently took the stage, and in an expressive baritone voice, filled the auditorium with William Blake's "Little Lamb":

Little lamb who made thee
Dost thou know who made thee...
Little lamb, I'll tell thee...
For He calls himself a Lamb...
Little Lamb, God bless thee.

What a blessing to witness success stories like that of Creshawn Smith—
the lost little lamb who found his voice, and a new way of life.

Antoinette Hollins (right) with
Laura Lathrop, Coordinator of the
Twin Cities ISP Women's Team

Antoinette Hollins
Twin Cities, MN

I am originally from Houston, Texas. My grandmother died when I was 15 years old, and I was forced to live with a family where I was unwanted. Seeking friendship and love in the wrong places, I fell into the wrong crowd. I began doing drugs and ultimately selling myself on the street. Drugs became the only medication I could find that eliminated my discomfort and feelings of being unwanted. I was on the street for 27 years. Eventually, I ended up in Minneapolis in a treatment program. My counselor suggested I attend an ISP retreat because I was struggling to restore my spirituality and find love and connection with God and community. I was so honored that they thought I would benefit from the retreat.

During the retreat, one of the team members, Laura, led a meditation. I had never meditated before. I thought, "I am gonna try this and see where it takes me." She told us to think of a quiet place of peace. I thought of the snow-covered mountain we had passed on our way to the retreat and the path that led to the top. During the meditation I felt freed. It was as though Jesus descended the peaceful mountaintop and told me everything would be alright. Now, whenever I need to find calm, I think of that quiet mountaintop that I first thought of during Laura's meditation. I have also found a wonderful friendship with Laura since we went on retreat together.

Since I have reconnected with my spirituality I have come to realize that there were many parts of my life I did not understand. As I have been able to reconnect with my God, I have been able to understand more clearly these parts of my life. My relationships with the women who were on retreat with me has encouraged me to continue on this path. I want to use this experience to become a role model for others who are having the same struggles and experiences.

All of us in the streets are looking for something. We are looking for love in all the wrong places. There are people out there who really do care. I found love in Minnesota on the ISP retreat. I am so happy and blessed that God has placed me on this journey. I was in the streets, into prostitution, and I want other women to know that there is a way out. I found it, through God.

PRAYING FOR WHAT WE MOST DEEPLY DESIRE

Fr. Nathan Wendt, SJ
Omaha, NE

"Where to now?" This question is asked near the conclusion of each overnight ISP retreat, and every time the question is asked I get the feeling of both nervousness and hope. The question is real. There are choices ahead. The question dares all retreatants to risk picking up the gift of trust we received during the retreat, and going forward—no longer alone and no longer in fear, but now with renewed dignity, being loved, having brothers, and with Jesus close by our sides.

I believe that faith and spirituality as practiced through Ignatian Spirituality and 12-step spirituality are essential means to ending homelessness in the USA. I have personally witnessed the salvation Christ offers through ISP retreats over the ten years I've been blessed in this ministry. I witness Christ's salvation for retreatants and I experience it myself as part of the ISP retreat team. It happens over and over again. Just as one example, I witnessed a retreatant realize through focused prayer that the abuse he suffered at the hands of his family as a child held him in bondage, keeping him from taking the necessary steps to freedom from deep self-doubt and crippling depression.

In his *Spiritual Exercises*, St. Ignatius asks us repeatedly to pray for what we want. At the beginning of each prayer, Ignatius asks the retreatant to ask God "for what I want and desire." ISP retreatants gain confidence in God's love to not only discover what they deeply desire, but also to ask God for it. I recall a retreatant discovering his deep desire for forgiveness from his daughter. He received courage and took the risk of seeking reconciliation, liberating his heart from guilt and opening his relationship to Christ's healing.

It is characteristic of ISP retreats that we are all making the retreat together—retreatants and facilitators alike. We are all praying to God for what we most deeply desire. I recall a retreat where I prayed for deeper joy in ministry as a Jesuit, to be liberated from pridefulness and fear of humiliation. I received great encouragement from the retreatants and left lifted up by God, allowing God's joy to reach me, as those accompanying me were experiencing that joy through me. With the Spirit's help, I am now overcoming this tendency to hide joy.

"Where to now?" I believe that ISP sends us out as a light, that we may be an "instrument of salvation to the ends of the earth" (Acts 13:47).

Fr. Nathan Wendt, SJ volunteered with ISP in Chicago and Boston during his formation to become a Jesuit priest. Ordained in 2014, he has since remained active with our ISP teams in Detroit and Omaha.

SPIRITUAL HEALING AND GROWTH

Ben Rubino
Milwaukee, WI

Although it may sound a bit cliché, it is no myth that the Lord works in mysterious ways. In 2012, fresh out of college, I moved to Milwaukee to begin a year of volunteer service with the Jesuit Volunteer Corps. I was placed at a daytime shelter, built on a model of self-governance, for men and women experiencing homelessness. The homeless community are charged with the tasks and duties of running the day-to-day operations of the center. On my first day, I walked into the shelter as the only individual who had never been homeless, and immediately a sense of uncertainty filled me. But my anxiety washed away almost as quickly as it overwhelmed me when I was welcomed by a man named Mark. He smiled and extended his hand saying, "Welcome Brother Ben," and with that I knew I would be okay.

Over the next few weeks, I settled in and my friendship with Mark grew. One day, I was explaining the Jesuit Volunteer Corps to Mark— Ignatian values, solidarity, spirituality, social justice, community—and I could see something connect in his mind. "That sounds a lot like these retreats I go on. You should come on one!"

The enthusiasm and light that radiated from Mark as he described the retreats made me want to join as soon as possible. It was apparent that the retreats that Mark was describing were life-changing for him and I wanted to share in those experiences. I didn't even know that retreats for homeless men and women existed or what they would be like, but that didn't matter. Mark sensed this and didn't delay. He picked up the shelter's phone, made a call, and just like that I started the process to join the ISP team!

I stayed in Milwaukee after ending my Jesuit Volunteer year and today, after three years, I proudly serve as the coordinator for the Milwaukee Men's Ignatian Spirituality Project team. My involvement with ISP has allowed me to continue to see Mark (who has transitioned from a retreatant to a witness to a member of the team) and foster spiritual healing and growth both in my life and the lives of dozens of men experiencing homelessness.

In most other instances, the recruitment process works the other way. A team member visits shelters and invites homeless men to make a retreat. Mine was the opposite. Cliché or not, I credit my experience and path to ISP to the Lord's mysterious works.

MY SPIRITUALITY HAS COME ALIVE

Judy M.
Boston, MA

I went on my very first ISP retreat in the spring of 2010. I remember that I was both excited and scared. When I look back on it, I remember how scary it was to sit in that circle of women. These were people I had just met and I didn't know how or what to share. It was a relief to discover that we all had so many things in common. After that first retreat, I felt like a new person—"renewal" is the word that comes to me. I found out things about myself that I didn't know, feelings that I didn't know I had. It was exciting and motivating.

I went to another ISP retreat about a year later. Since then, I've been a witness at two ISP retreats. I was a total wreck the first time I gave my witness statement. I wondered how my story could help anybody else. I shared the story of my alcoholism with the group, telling them how my desire for recovery led me to separate from my husband in 1997, although it took eight more years for me to get and stay sober. During that time, my husband committed suicide in 2005. Then in 2009, my 30-year-old son also committed suicide. At that time, I had been sober three years, and I am proud of the fact that, even with the shock and pain of my son's death, I did not go back to drinking.

I'm not used to thinking of myself as a leader, but giving that witness statement showed me that I can give hope to others, and this motivated me as much as the group.

My best friend of 42 years died a year after my son. I think about what she would say about me now since I've done these retreats. I think, first of all, she would be proud of me. I think she would also say, "Judy has turned over a new leaf. She's willing to share, is more outgoing, and is just a more positive person."

I went back to college when I was 57 years old. I enrolled in a women's program, "Choices, Challenges and Change." I think now that that is what life really is, and I have made positive choices, have risen to challenges, and I have truly changed. I'm in a job training program, and working as a receptionist at a YMCA. Although I was estranged from my daughter, I'm now very close to her, her husband, and my four grandchildren. I love being a grandma. If my best friend could see me now, she would say, "Judy's face has been beaming for two years!"

What have the ISP retreats done for me? I like to say that I've had a spiritual awakening. Between Alcoholics Anonymous and ISP, my spirituality has come alive. I try to do the right thing, I take one day at a time, and I try to keep the past in the past, and let myself heal. Every time I share my story I keep my spirit renewed. It's funny; I didn't really think I had a "story." Sharing it has taught me that I do, and that it can help others. Telling it helps me accept who I am and keeps me motivated. I'm enlightened myself every time I tell it. When I think of that first ISP retreat, I think of the word "renewal" and my spirit still feels renewed every time I go on a retreat. The sharing of my story has brought me totally out of my shell, and lets me see the bigger and better picture of what life has to offer!

A SPIRITUAL
AWAKENING

Bruce Meyer
Cincinnati, OH

I was born in Cincinnati in a middle class neighborhood with two loving parents and eight brothers and sisters. It was a pretty big family but we really never wanted for anything. My mom was a nurse at a nursing home, and was a user of prescription drugs. But I don't remember my parents drinking alcohol much.

I was 17 the first time I remember drinking. I drank a whole fifth of rum and I thought it was really neat. It helped me fit in. I was a skinny guy at school, I was little, I had pimples, I was kind of shy, so I always got chased and beat up and things like that. When I entered college I drank only on weekends, more as a recreation. But when I graduated from nursing school my drinking really took off because I had two or three days off in a row and I had the money to buy whatever I wanted.

I got married in 1983. I told my wife when we were dating that I thought I was an alcoholic. She later said she didn't believe me and didn't know what an alcoholic was. She found out first-hand. Shortly after our wedding she was pregnant and I was sick with the flu. She went off to work and I proceeded to go out and buy two bottles of gin and drink both bottles in an afternoon. She told me I needed help and I agreed. I didn't want to start a new life with a new child, a new wife and a new house, being an alcoholic. So I went to a treatment center and stayed sober for eight years.

It was when my dad died that I relapsed. Being a nurse, I was really involved with his care. I was there when he drew his last breath and I was the one who pronounced him dead. I was very stoic during the funeral and everything, I didn't cry. I thought I had to be the strong man. It was three months later—I remember I had 99 months sober—when I relapsed. I found myself at a liquor store and figured since I'm here, I might as well get something to drink. I drank half a fifth before I got back home. Because I hadn't grieved I had built this up. There was no warning at all, it just happened suddenly, like the car drove itself to that liquor store. I only relapsed a short period that time, only a matter of months. I had another string of two years, went to treatment, another string of three or four years, went into treatment, and so on, until I had deteriorated so much that I was starving. I was 40 pounds underweight. I was starting to have seizures, starting to have blackouts, things that hadn't happened before. I was also involved in drugs at this time. Being a nurse I had easy access to them.

At that point my wife of 18 years divorced me. I lost my wife, my kids, my house, my car, all at the same time. Then my drinking really took off. I thought, "Heck, I'm alone now, there's nobody to gripe about it, nobody to hide it from." It got to the point where I couldn't even function on my own. I had no coherent thoughts. I couldn't make up my mind to do anything. The laundry never got done. I was too confused to pick out a different set of clothes, so I wore the same clothes all the time. Every once in a while I'd say, "I wonder when I took a shower last." My brother, who I was renting an apartment from, came over one day and he said, "You're going to a treatment center." I agreed and I went into the program on February 11, 2014. I never thought I'd live to see my one-year anniversary. I had given up on life, I didn't care if I lived or died. I'd started getting in trouble with the law.

At the treatment center I heard about the ISP retreat and asked if I could go. I knew I was lacking in spirituality; I had no Higher Power at that point. I distrusted God, I couldn't pray to God and consequently He just wasn't part of my life. I was raised Catholic, but the prayers that I learned, like the Hail Mary, were just words—I didn't think about what I was saying. I knew that something was missing and when I heard it was a spirituality retreat, I said, "Yeah, that's what I need. I need spirituality." I asked my counselor, who selected somebody else out of our group. But I was the alternate. And God saw fit to send me. The first guy couldn't come and I got selected. That was what I needed when I needed it.

On the retreat in Milford, Ohio I had a spiritual awakening. I'd been drinking for 40 years by this time and I just couldn't process the word "God." Early in the morning on the second day of the retreat, I woke up and I said, "Thank you, God, for letting me be here. I really learned something. I learned that the spirit and spirituality is all around me, whether it be in the person next to me or the tree outside." Then I thought how grateful I was for being here to experience this upwelling of feeling. It wasn't until later on that day I thought, "Wow, that was a spiritual awakening." I had such a vision that I prayed, and I'd never prayed like that before. It was like an energy, like a bolt of lightning hit me, "Wow!" It taught me how to pray with my Higher Power, and He's my friend now. Before He was some deity up in the sky and the reason I prayed to Him was so I don't go to Hell. What spirituality is all about to me now is being a whole person and willing to help other people. It's praying in your own way, it's meditation. Whether it be riding a bicycle, driving a car, taking a shower, when you consciously reach out to God and say, "Thank you for this day," or "Can you help me with this?" or "I really appreciate what you did over here." That's what it's all about. That's what I got from the retreats I went on. I just thank God that I was able to do that.

After the retreat, people started saying stuff to me about how much I was changing, about how I was becoming a role model, how I'd had all these significant changes in myself, and I'm going, "What are you talking about? I still feel terrible, I look terrible." I didn't see it at first, but they did. Something had started changing and I know it now.

I was a loner, and when I first got to the treatment center I still isolated myself. When I came back from the retreat I felt rejuvenated to the point that I was gradually able to interact a little bit. I had the ability now to pray to a Higher Power which really relieved my soul. Other people used to really piss me off quite frequently. But after the retreat I thought, it really doesn't matter. I know that somebody loves me, my God loves me. I could talk to Him now and just lay this burden at His feet. That's what I chose to do. The retreat made a big difference to me because I wasn't as angry as I had been. I learned to accept things better. I was firmly rooted into something.

Since the retreat I'm dreaming again. I had long rejected the idea of being a counselor, but now I'm preparing an application to be an addictions counselor, to help out other alcoholics.

Interested in learning more about how to champion, engage or invest in ISP's ministry? Please get in touch!

Ignatian Spirituality Project
1641 South Allport Street
Chicago, IL 60608
(312) 226-9184

info@ispretreats.org

www.ignatianspiritualityproject.org
www.youtube.com/c/ignatianspiritualityproject1

Many thanks to all of our generous volunteers and staff whose efforts continue to touch the lives of so many through ISP retreats. Special thanks to those who contributed their stories to this collection.